TIME

AND

CHANCE

TIME AND CHANCE

KATHARINE COLES

Turtle Point Press
Brooklyn, New York

Requests for permissions to make copies of any
part of the work should be sent to:
Turtle Point Press, 208 Java Street, Fifth Floor,
Brooklyn, NY 11222
info@turtlepointpress.com

Library of Congress Cataloguing-in-Publication Data
Names: Coles, Katharine, author.
Title: Time and chance / Katharine Coles.
Description: First edition. | Brooklyn, New York : Turtle Point Press, 2025.
Identifiers: LCCN 2025004332 (print) | LCCN 2025004333 (ebook)
ISBN 9781885586681 (paperback) | ISBN 9781885983909 (ebook)
Subjects: LCGFT: Poetry.
Classification: LCC PS3553.O47455 T56 2025 (print)
LCC PS3553.O47455 (ebook) | DDC 811/.54--dc23/eng/20250221
LC record available at https://lccn.loc.gov/2025004332
LC ebook record available at https://lccn.loc.gov/2025004333

Design by Joan Wong

Print ISBN: 978-1-885586-68-1
eBook ISBN: 978-1-885983-90-9

First Edition
Printed in the United States of America

For Joan Coles, 1932-2022

Don't worry. I'll still be in your head.

CONTENTS

1. Dream of Flight

1. Dream of Flight

ADVENT

Light a candle. Open a door
Too small to walk through. In

The already not yet, a voice
Calls from the woods: barely

Sounding bird or bobcat, a fawn
Like the one we cut loose from the fence

Six months ago, its mother a shadow
Still among trees. Now

When we step outside she doesn't
Startle but lifts her head

And keeps chewing. It was the hymns
My mother loved, singing

Come, then waiting. Listening, we flash
Lights down the mountain. The cry

Becomes silence. Maybe
Comfort has arrived. Maybe not.

While I floated,

My mother sang arias – to me,
To herself, we didn't always know.
On a good day "O Mio
Babbino Caro," on another

"Dido's Lament," or, while she
Danced us through Carmen's dark
Habanera, "L'amour est un oiseau
rebelle." Later, her voice

Rose through the house, the Met's
Saturday live broadcast
Singing along on the radio. By
Then, I could softly shut my door,

But during those months inside,
She told me later, I kicked her hard.

LITTLE SOUND

The owl's body opens a door. Her face
Listens. She watches with ears that figure
Angles and distance, her cochlea
Gigantic; inside the aperture you'd see

Her eyes' binocular tubes reach all
The way back. Following me in the dark or
Through closed lids, she delivers
Messages between worlds, between

Inside the shell where her owlet begins
Singing and the mother it sings to, the
Out there out here. Sometimes she flies
So close I abandon my senses,

Her wings slicing, soundless,
Muffled with velvet. Unmoved, the air.

The apple flies while standing still,

Hovering high in a tree
Otherwise bare of fruit, leaves,
Even birds – or if a sparrow lights
No one has realized her yet, since

A sparrow landing means nothing
We need to notice, not even
A bird on a branch. A cedar waxwing
Becomes herself her flight, each

Little bone the world has made: she
Like the apple flies apart and remains
Intact. Why should she not settle
If a tree offers only a place to sit,

No apples; why not tuck her beak
And dream her dream of flight?

ATOM

The smallest Medieval measure of time
The OED says, *the twinkling of*

– whose eye? Dickinson was female too
Early to imagine microscopically,

Though she did, and also
Described herself in dim

-inutives, as I do myself, though
A man will like as not correct me.

.

.

PHOTON

Like everything, we fly
At lightspeed – charging past
Each other so fast you
Can't catch my eye, only

An idea I've lost
Before I grasp it. Is it the same
For you? I never did get carsick:
However rutted the road

I'd bury my head in a book
And leave my stomach
Behind. In motion as I am,
I can't worry about what I know

Only in abstraction, though
It thrills me through.

When you invent gravity

You hold me so hard
I have to remember I travel

Even stuck in place. What I

See of the future gleams
And waffles, detached

Vitreous I look past to focus

Out there. Easy not to lever
Myself from my chair, knowing

I'm going everywhere.

The physicist

1. performs without
Notes. His laptop projects gravity
Bending a grid while earth

And moon roll on dizzy
Repeat through its hairpins
And hillocks. I ride his models

Past into future then past
Again, where a clunky equation gets
2. Whittled down then Einstein

Adds two others – already
Exquisitely compact – making one
So powerful it curves space, arrays

Mass, manifests our universe as
What must be. Now flashes
An image I take

A second to realize is a screen
-saver: ethereal forest, snow-
covered, a glitch. Still

3. Talking, he restarts
And the screen blanks until
Some algorithm recovers trees

And snow, and losing not one
Syllable he clicks a key to bring
Forth more numbers. The way

He carries them, his arms
Graceful and emphatic,
Persuades me. Over dinner, he says

        4. He once believed mathematics
Existed before mind, the universe,
Even time, which math gave

No choice but being. When
My friend the mathematician, still
A Platonist, asks what changed

His mind, he says back then
        5. He didn't care the universe
Will end. He has a daughter, twelve

I think, a son. Grief approaches as
Pinprick and wave. He hopes
The math is wrong. What would I feel

If the universe considered my
Love for it? – having never imagined
Words could predict reality, much

Less bring it on, and not just
Conjure every little thing
My mind obliges me to see.

COMPLICATIONS

The tourbillon. The perpetual
Calendar. Subdials and timers

And ornamental whirligigs
I need not to use

But to have: push a button
And a window opens

A singular view I admire
Then click shut. Time

Enough to ask whether
I really know what

Elaborate design can
Make me keep it on.

Color has evolved more than once

And lets a parrot feel more
Than I feel: Descartes

Teaches me what color is

Primary. My eyeball's
Apparatus can't make a rainbow

Even with its fragile photo

-receptive cones and rods, but
The machine they talk to

Deep in my head assembles red

Peonies and a sky scattering light
Blue all over. Inside, my brain

Reinvents Descartes fanning

His wing to show off ultraviolets
I can't see, though even for me

Green feathers pop against a white

Wall and complement my friend's
Painting of imaginary fronds

And leaves close up, greens

She moves around as paint. Making
Himself at home, Descartes says

Hi sweetie, and his voice

Touches me inside, caressing
My cochlear cilia. He and I

Don't see with our ears

Though together we
Attune to the hawk's call

Falling from so high I can't yet

Descry her. As Descartes
Has taught me, I tilt my head,

One eye scanning the sky.

Who sees,

Who gets to be

Seen? Sargent unfurls
Another woman in satin

Or diamonds; he pink

-tips her ears, trails
Feathers. The way a shoulder

Slopes – I tell myself

Look. Older now, I array
Myself as usual in black

Patent and trousers, jacket

Softest red or black again,
Embroidered flowers

Straying white and green

Down the placket. Friends
Also show up as them

-selves: cargo pants, polos,

A different earth
-color every day. Usually

Serious, I decide to become

Something im-
practical: a newly

Fluffed-up cloud, blues

Skiffing the walkways,
A hint of bruise. *Beauty, what*

Can I make you? Being

Only my late
-lingering eye,

A trailing-after sigh.

DEGAS DANCERS

The animal of them gauzes
And abstracts, skirts

Emitting light in clouds. For us
Through him they remain beasts

Plowing the studio's field. In this
Degas differed from none: he blocked

Bodies to make them
Work for him. The men come into

Paint differently, the *Nabis* not daubed
And frivolously lit but wearing dark

Suits, poised to speak, drawn
To blow the world

Up. Not like these
Assemblages of legs and arms,

Akimbo as you like, those
Breasts, those lazy eyes, that hair.

AFTERNOON LECTURE

On the lawn, a statue of a kangaroo
Becomes a kangaroo. Others
Show up – a duo, a few
More – and grazing fills the glass

Wall I haven't let distract me
But a moment, maybe
When a cloud floated over then
Squalled so hard its raindrops

Bounced. The kangaroos, noses
Absorbed in wet grass, don't fly or hop
But laze across my view,

Intent. Once, I told a man
Who chided me, *I always*
Pay attention. Just not to you.

SKYWRITING

1. The plane turns up
-side-down and loop-
de-loops poor Joe's question,
Unable to hold its ache

One more second for Giselle
-Miranda, whose name
In cursive must have cost him
A nickel or two: *Will*

you? The *what* waits to emerge
While a cloud smudges
The sky's blue board: down

Here, will we see the magic
Words, will she, before
It all blows over?

2. I want to know
Like everyone: how
Do they climb so high? Those

Perpetrators of LA
Hip, *like spiders weaving*
Forty floors up and more (*This*

Is the problem of the city): imagine
Color and form against
The sky, then paint it – no gallery

More urban, no graffiti
Harder to scrub off. Who
Wants to? Who's for

And who against *Tolt*
And *Rakm*, *Shaak* – or is it
Shark? – and *Eels*, surfing

Signature waves that cloud and break
Up in the air where before
There was just a real

-estate deal gone bad. Not street-
But skyscape more *vibrant*
Than the bankrupt developers

Planned. *Now you gotta do*
A whole building, CES says. *This*
Eclipses. I think of their

Flights, as they call them, scaling floor
By floor with spray-paint: only stair

-wells, no stairs. *People do whatever*
They want, a neighborhood
Coffee-shop owner says. The dizzy

Ascent, the thirst. I want to see it before
Someone scrubs it off. If only I could
Fly up there myself.

A NOTE ON THE APPARENT LOWERING OF MORAL STANDARDS IN THE LEPIDOPTERA

I could tell them apart,
But why? I know
What they are
After, frolicking, mud

-puddling, rolling thoraxes
And wading in pollen, leaving
Fine and dusted. I would

Not blame them for rooting –
A proboscis won't hurt
A bit – or for what they scatter

As they fly off. Their flutter
Holds time mid-air
And long, making whatever
Feels best last.

By no means something in general,

1\. a wing presents
Itself, *identical with nature.* Is
It also *the real*
World unfolding green
Feather, yellow
Down? I can't take
A journey into my own
Image projecting that wing

2\. opening, no farther. Himself
Overthought, parrot
Descartes feels full of words
Wanting to fly. He says
Descartes, esses
Silent. He says *I am*, or
Iamb. He calls out, calls
In, *What's your name?* Answers
Himself, *Descartes.* Hangs himself
Upside-down, sometimes still
Poised sometimes in full
Swing, green orange yellow
Moved by something I'd name
Delight if I could know
He swings because he is

3. suspended between
Destination and idea,
Solid ground and cloud
Sunrise fires through so
It shape-shifts, becomes
Shredlets, then changes
Names. Fire joins him briefly in
Flash and rumble, alarms
His nerve sounds flitting
High into desire. What

4. -ever may fix it, he
Is no machine, has
No gears to grind, no cogs
Spinning or thirst for oil
Or off switch: when he goes
It's lights out. He knows
His life thrums through him, runs
Him as he runs: he rings
His bell and wants
An answer. If this means
He has *an immortal soul*, or
Is one, don't ask him. "I" am
Not his problem.

If past becomes future

Under their fast sky, some still
Will flit, clever bodies and light

Invisible among the leaves – or,

If their trees have not
Returned, some will burrow

Or bower; some winkle from

The roots of grasses bugs that also
Escaped, and seeds, or learn to sip new

Nectars dreamed up by what flowers

Become. Those blooms, insects, whatever
Birds call themselves, wear colors

We can't imagine, not that we see

The world well now, having never before
Needed accurate vision. Consider who

We mourn in advance. We grew up

Alongside, on them cultivated
Love for heart-catch and grandeur,

Named them. When we go,

Who do the small and quick fan
Their wings for, flashing eyes? Who do

They preen for now?

PINANGA SUBTERRANEA

If you open your petals
Underground, your flowers un-
furl in hiding and glow as they will
Only for themselves until someone

Brushes the dirt away. Not new
To yourself, you don't like being
Tasted, or maybe you've
Had more fondling than

You want and can't stand any
Strange eye touching you. Days
Feel like that: my head

Sunk deep inside opens me,
Old to itself in layers laid down,
A valley buried under clouds.

ARTICHOKE

They came out of some
-where, those tight-wound
Globes in the produce section, but

This plant might have
Landed from space, taller
Than I am and arms out

-spindling to send me all
Directions at once, each wrist
breaking into a new time

And place: here a bud not yet
Open, there a blossom bright
Purple and so sexed-out in the sun

Bees can't help themselves, get
Drunk and burrow in to feel
Tiny petals caressing them

All over, little legs scrabbling
Every which way. Then
Look here: fruit

Has plumped out all but
Ripe, its blush pinking so
I keep my eyes right on it.

OCTOBER

We fell not out of Eden
But into it – can't fall
Farther. My husband, loving

Deer and rhododendrons, plants
The latter though the former
Will nip every bud short of blossom,

The doe leading her fawns
Ricketing thin legs from the gully
And under our noses

Showing them what tastes most
Delectable. He digs three
-foot holes and carries his beautiful

Faith through the world. He turns
A bramble-covered slope to make
Milkweed for butterflies, beard

-tongue for hummingbirds, lavender
And *they-don't-call-it-bee*
-balm for nothing, he says, for

Guess who. In spring, he's sure,
Winged bodies will bear forth
Their hunger, then drink before

Lifting from yellow throats, done
And dusted. He won't pray for creatures
Falling on us from the sky. Fall

They must. It's the future
He believes in: the air still
Alive, and so, so much perfume.

The lifespan of a mosquito

looks like real
-ity out of focus
Until it moves, her wings

Beating time so fast
I hear it hum. Like me
She seems the world
She needs. Should be hard,

Imagining a life so
Small also a life big as all
A body senses. The male
Smells nectar, honeydew,

Plant sap. The female
Smells my blood.

NOT ONE THING

Living deep in this
Body, mind being
Distraction. Always

Reach for whatever, thorn
-stemmed rose or gorgeously
Fingered frog who may
Sweat poison. Why not trick

Out my fingertips
And suction myself
Hard to a leaf among

Droplets I am small
Enough to sip. Fill, then
Founder. In time I will

Have nothing left to touch,
Nothing to touch it with.

I am here to stop your heart,

Rothko never said. A stanza builds
A chapel: walls, ceiling, floor,
And anywhere you turn the dark
Arrests. Stand wherever and gravity

Works or fails until you fall
Open. My heart keeps itself
Locked in a vaulted cathedral.
It can stop a hundred

-thousand times a day, stops
Whenever it unclenches, and
Every pause becomes another
Surge. I lie down, a bewildered

Beast turned loose in me, deep
Red and ravenous. Still, I sleep.

RETURN

Dropping in after a long absence
I find a door on the latch or a lock
Easy pickings; might notice
An oven still warm, the smell

Of bread or flesh roasting.
The bedroom holds its own
History: the late-night
Nod, a shout trailed by a kiss

And what follows that, a window
Thrown open to night's softening. Out
There in the trees, birds settle
Gently or call into the dark. I wonder

What colors they wear in daylight,
What jewels brighten their wings.

DEER AT NIGHT

They drift while we dream.
Slow ghosts among the trees
Pause to drink at the fountain.

Last night our camera's
Night-vision caught them – but they
Escape the frame, so *caught* can't be
The right word. The doe

Recrosses the screen, trailing two
Fawns, nearly grown now. Last spring,
I held one of them in my arms, his
Body a tremor I felt through mine

But couldn't see. *Slow*, I lifted him free,
Wanting to cause no further harm.
She stood just there and watched me.

2. Ghost

ROOM IN AN OLD HOTEL

If you heard what happened
You would never picture

Beamed ceilings and wallpaper depicting
Old-fashioned hunting scenes,

An off-white field of birds. You wouldn't
Think of arched doorways

Leading to bathroom and closet
(And closet, and closet, and closet)

Or the kitchenette equipped
With two of everything

You might in those days have needed. The room
Had bookshelves built into the walls

And doors you'd now call
Original, French windows

Open to nonspecific palm trees.
The people across the grass

Had words, despair, malice
Aforethought, or only bodies

Clumsy with good intentions.
Think how much blood.

In a million years
You wouldn't have imagined.

DREAM OF FORGETFULNESS

All he was at twenty-seven.
Sixteen, all she'd ever be.
They could have had any bodies, one
Taken, the other giving way.

Still, I don't believe in spirits. Only air
Moves the curtains. It nests in the attic
And flashes through ancient electrics
Sparking the wires. That flicker

Rises from some quirk of weather
Passing like a pulse with nowhere
Else to go. It carries me like thought,
Sweet and heavy. It is no more.

GHOST

When I speak your name. When you
Borrow my tongue. When you draw
Me down a shaded path in dream

Or float in my eye. The corner
Where you sat in the kitchen
No longer ours. The green

Hills of summer. A chill falls
No different from the last.
This time, it never leaves.

TWO BLOWS

First, my mother
Slaps me. Next,
I slap her back.

All these years
Later, both sting: my
Face, my hand.

LIFE LESSON

Learn to live with death
And die. Take your loss
To bed. Let it lie.

BRIDGE

I lit no match. It was always
Going up, isn't that what sun
Does to us and time's long
Wind rounding the horizon, another

Dawn eating us alive. I'd known
All this, but I hadn't heard
Flames crack just in my ear's
Hollow, turning sound to space

Where a woman stood, her one
Body bridging a present and a past,
Both specific, now lost. *I'll ask*

Her, I think. But she can't answer
Or even echo back my words.
No sound I know can fill that air.

Death

props up every
Wall, lounges around

The corners; death
Ambles, of course, fixing

His gaze. Meanwhile,
Not imagining myself to be

Out of range exactly, I also
Fail to find myself

Well in sight, the bulls
-eye right here.

ENDURANCE

So long since I thought of ghost
-ships underwater, intact

Hulls naming themselves in shots
Too clear to believe. Shackleton's men all
Survived, still with us from the lost

Heroic age we feel in 2020
We understand, though we move

So slowly and count our dead
As well as we can, no more. Remember
The early days, ships trapped

Not by ice but in what we call
Harbor, sick and dying held aboard

So near home they could
Wave from their portholes. If we
Return, caught in a circular current, how

Can we spin free? How,
Frozen in time, go on.

LIMNOLOGY

When a lake vanishes
It might rise again elsewhere
Out of thin air to haunt you. It
Swears to return as rain, to fall

Elsewhere then rise again, but
Time waits for its keeping –
You swear, you've seen no rainfall
This year to the next. Maybe

A lake keeps time, outwaiting
Drought, sky, thought,
Decade by decade. Maybe, if
Two lakes count their time

In floods, the sky forgets
It can't return the same lakes.
Two lakes keeping time
Become something else again,

Might return as one lake,
Ghostly pale, grey-green.
It becomes something else, again
Overwhelming its hollow—

A water-green ghost and pale
Or a tin-foil shimmer of heat.
Can it sink again? How low?
Questions beg to be asked: *What*

Metal, what shimmer, what heat?
Don't count how many
Questions beg for your asking. If
Memory haunts you, or ghost,

Don't wonder how
Water becomes thin air. What
Haunts you, ghost or memory,
When the lake vanishes?

MEMORY CARE

I remember every day
My father in his wheelchair raising

His eyes from wherever he was

Keeping inside himself. I hope
The scene shimmers

Clear and radiant, maybe

A mountainside deep in snow
He labors to scale, stalking

A buck he carries only

His camera to shoot, no longer
Needing to feed his family. The buck

In my father's photo frames

Himself on the ridge in silhouette
While my father creeps so close

He smells animal musk, a body his

Animal self wants to haul back
Down the mountain. He's glad this time

He carries the buck inside a little box

He can pocket. The rose sunset
Has already faded, and he must track

Himself back through the snow, deep

Down the moonless canyon
Alone.
              Where was I?
                                    Oh yes,

I am walking in the door and he

Lifts his eyes and catches me
There looking, both outside

The drift of new snow and inside,

And though he isn't meant to know
Who I am now, his gaze fixes me

And his eyes fill with light.

GHOST WAY

If a ribcage could carry his
Heartbeat and running banjo,
Mandolin's wood, his voice

Strung high in a nose made,
We said, to amplify, then a lake
Whispering while we fished may

Or may not still exist, and the blind
Sheet of ice that fed it, even then
Pulling back. He could be quiet

As all that when he wanted,
And is. His bandurria and lutes
Sit on my shelf, dusty and gone

Ornamental, composing
Themselves a bridge I won't cross
Or a shrine I pass and sometimes

Notice. I remember a voice
Carries across water. I keep
His in my head with all those

Souvenirs and scraps
Unswept, drifting, adding up
The way I go, we all do.

If my father dreams of me,

I am the lake diminished to
Its farthest point and lowest,

He the salt left on a late
High shoreline drying, just

One marking the foothills
Where for 30,000 years the lake kept

Lapping as it fell. Are
You there? May as well

Ask does a dead sea keep
Imagining – it does

When I imagine it. Dead
Meaning every place

Left to go, while
Generations of birds fly in one

Long moment then light among
The reeds and rushes, so

Constant, calling one to another
I am coming in, still coming.

THREE DREAMS

1. Over lunch at Pierre's, Mark chats as usual: poetry, food and wine, his new shoes whose deep brown leather will only improve with time.

"They're Italian," he tells me.

Every so often, he waves his hand and says, "Let's let that go."

Finally, I ask, "What?"

He gleams again, in that way he had, and says, "Everything, of course."

2. I have come to New York to study witchcraft, which, the dream tells me, requires intricacy, flair, the right words in the right order, and performance.

I am called to an overcrowded auditorium to give a reading I never knew about or had forgotten. Are they all there for me? I leaf through a sheaf of poems in disarray. When I drop them, scattering, Larry appears on the floor beside me and begins to pick them up, approving some, setting others aside. As ever, he is bemused, low key, utterly calm. He mentions he is meant to be reading with me.

I wonder, then, if instead of poems, I should read an essay.

He says, "Well, I am *supposed* to read, but of course I can't."

"Why not?" I ask.

He levels his long, chill gaze on me, and says, "I'm dead."

3. I am walking, the west on fire behind me. I drop down into a valley green with spring. Inside a low fence, a whole garden blooms. The breeze blows clean and fresh.

Through the one tiny window of a cottage with no doors in its walls, I see my father lying on a narrow bed, a white handkerchief covering his face. I knock on the glass, and he lifts the cloth and smiles.

I gesture *Come along*, but he waves, as if to say, *You go ahead.*

I do.

The day eighty

suddenly looked young,
A poem by my old teacher
Rose from the grave, wafting within it

His dream of that longer-gone poet
He'd rousted out of whatever dim
Dive the great dead lounge

Around in, shedding sparks
And scraps of paper, admiring
One another's footwear. This

Is what we mean by
Immortality, though Mark
Can have no idea, nine years

Gone, he has shimmered back
Exactly into my light: page
62 of *The New Yorker*, where

He was always showing up
During his lifetime, regular
And sonorous as his voice

Striking. Writing this
Resurrection, did he feel himself
Dying? More than usual,

I mean. When I married
He gave me knives I still
Sharpen up. *Someday, you might*

Need them, he said. Twenty-one,
In painting school when Stevens died, Mark
Must have met him only in black

And white, the way one voice slides
Itself into another and fits. The wave
Enfolds them both, Mark's voice

An echo lifting, raising Stevens'
Again to echo him. Of course, nobody
Has caught the *one idea*, but

Imagine those two riding it
Side-by-side from deep water
All the way in, to shore.

FAMILY SNAPS

1. Too many show small
Figures walking away
Into cliffs and skies over
There. A distance beckons

While a man and woman
Naked under a waterfall
Lose their faces in foam

And tumult – or someone
Squeezes sideways to chimney
A slot canyon, knees and elbows
Strategically deployed, eyes

Turned not our way but toward
The problem. These people
Knew the limits of posing

2. And aiming, so devoted
Themselves to a body's
Dynamics and every science
Engaging locomotion,

Friction, geometry, how
Fast they would become
Weightless. Given

You can't tell them
Apart by how they threw
Or carried their lives
Away, you never will

Know them. Look: the camera
Cuts her off at the knees,
Casts his shoulder and arm and

3. Half a face into some
Other dimension – blame
Not the machine but
A human eye, its focus

On distractions out
-side the frame. Here, a
Crease and blur; there,

A tear. We thought
We might see all the way
Back to find them, then
Send them forward, but

We can't even say where
These bodies, caught
Up and still, have gone.

BEAUTY

Say my mother was
One absolutely, camera
-caught in the mirror holding

Lipstick to her smile or scaling
A sheer cliff with that guy
She never trusted belaying

The rope, though he wouldn't
Let go and she can't fall
Now. The photo reduces

Her to palm-size, so
You might take her in
Hand. Later, some other fellow

Will pose her for the news, coiffed
And already lipsticked, holding
Her rock hammer to her face

As if she wants to kiss it. Such
A strange idea. When instructed,
She smiles cold-eyed as any

Gas-station calendar girl. See her
Pretending she won't use
The pick end if she has to.

Still angry

about something
He might have said but didn't,

She twisted her mouth that way
And decided not to forgive him

This either. He had done
More than enough. So

She looked after her
-self, quarreling with the world

She loved and made
Us all live in.

I can't watch

a moon rise in her –
Too pale, riding
The window's blue,

Blue sky. Holding her hand
And watching her work over
What she becomes, I know

Why we say *gravely*
Ill – she lies a few
Hours from learning who

Came out right, who wrong.
She's dying to know.
For now, she drifts, eyes

A-swim and spangly
As a crystal ball I see
So far into, never through.

Then the moon falls

face-first into the lake. The sun
Will rise too late to shed
More light than a Hunter's Moon
Burns: the sun sits out of sight

Just *there* to shine the moon
So bright. *Nothing in her life*
Became – meaning
She grows luminous in her

Leaving, now we see
Her go. If she could, she might
Say she's loving her fall
Headlong, too late

Too fast to stop. There sinks
The moon, fierce and hunting. Here,
The sun flashes, over
-brimming. Last-minute

Nobody knows what to do
With how change
Happens, everyone suddenly
Switching roles. The script

Demands we speak the lines
Given, not those we've tossed off
All our lives. If she can
We can, right? And will.

COMEDY in three poems

1. *Where you go for the company, not the climate,*

My grandmother used to call the state
Where she retired to watch the sunset, over
-the-yard-arm whisky in her left hand, in her right
A cube of Wisconsin cheese. Later, we toured

The supermarket lot in her Nova, my Virgil
Gossiping about the dead – all her old circle
Wicked-fast like her. She cornered
Hard, cocking an eye for a cart to walk

Her into the store, all the while
Speculating like an old Italian which long
-dead beaux and rivals would have ended

Where, given what trials for their errors.
Where she landed I haven't nerve to wonder.
I only wish her the best in conversation.

2. The Late Middle

Who knew this would be so much work?
Dash through a curtain of fire, rinse,
Repeat. I thought I'd just have to wait,
Swinging my foot and tapping the table, not

Dash through curtains of fire. Rinse
Then wire my eyes shut so they can't devour
A swinging Manolo, jeweled fingers tapping
A lyric I can't get out of my head. It makes me

Long to wire my ears shut. Already, I can't see
Through the smoke rings I blow
Trying to clear my head, that make me
Want to flip my lid or lie down. What with

All the smoke I have to blow
I'm too busy huffing around to chat
Or let off steam or have a lie-down. Given
Everything bitter takes its own sweet time

I'm too busy counting down to chat;
And if I too much love the world's offerings –
Campari, sweet dreams – I take
What's all good to have but not to want,

Or want too much of. What earth offers
Binds me to it and makes me dust.
What is good: to have, but not to want;
All is good to have, except desire

Binds me to it. If dust makes flesh,
A peach hangs out of reach. What makes dust?
Good to have but not desire to get
The mouth around – everything. Dangle

Out of reach the dust-made peach,
The body's fruits the poets sing to get
Their mouths around: every damned thing
I should not have touched. Wanting

Them, I mouthed them into song. Get,
Repeat. I thought I'd mostly have to wait,
Trying not to touch what I could reach.
Who knew that would be so much work?

3. *As usual, I was going to skip Paradise,*

famously changeless and full of instruction,
When close over the eaves rough-danced
The pair of Cooper's hawks keeping house
Nearby – lofting over the canyon

Half-tumbling up and up to get at each other,
Touching wings and breasts, holding talons
And beaks away from tender bellies,
Deploying rough-body caress in dalliance

As they rose. If later they light from wilderness
Of air, if sun, wind, and sinew bear
Their hollow bones into summer, if the nest

They line with their own breast-down
Holds, chicks will hatch and call, fledge
And also fly. It will happen here.

WILL

The past spins faster than ever.
It leaves us behind.

Fall comes then has come,
And we ride along.

Where do we live now
She has left us to it,

Who never took tea from a cup
Too good for everyday use?

Too good for the everyday
She took tea from a cup

Someone drank from once,
A century gone, from

Another box, its plates
Wrapped up in old news.

SESTINA IN PROSE: THREE DREAMS

Even as they unfold, I don't believe three dreams can fit in one, though all three take my head at once left and right: far, up close. See where on the left, in black and white, I pack a big box

with little boxes, believing I must notch each shape in precisely, without gaps. My mother left no instructions, though I see each box finds space just where

I put it – not like in this other dream, where I bury little boxes in a big one burgeoning with shreds of paper and can't see where they go. I believe paper flies into feathers, thousands, though how could that be? I am left

hands-full of softness, left nothing here, though my hands burrow through unfathomable fluff. Those little boxes, where did they get to? I can't leave this black-and-white but I see

tufts burgeon, see left-over eider drift into
a third dream, the same, where I believe
pink and yellow flowers will bloom, ex-
travagances of blue, so they do. I wander,
strewing little boxes, though

what do they hold? – though I can no lon-
ger see a box once I've left it, nestled un-
der hydrangea, primrose, peony, gone not
to feathers but flowers, graveyards being
neither there nor here. I believe

Some point was there to be made, though
I could only see it, not make it. Waking, I
left three dreams adrift where they leave
me, unboxed, beyond believing.

Relic,

not relict, though she was orphaned then widowed before she left me, not so much over as at a loss. You could say I remain to break trail or bear the wind's force for whoever follows; who knew how strong the gale was or how she kept taking it, out there alone in front. I remember her standing apart on top of one peak and also another, letting the rope dangle or pulling it up behind her, coiling it hand-to-elbow. Did she live in profile, her most elegant pose, or had she already started to turn herself away? What life leaves you, she knew, remains another question, and another. Her life left her, as she threatened, *in my head*; in my head it keeps me trying to breathe as she did, steady in every high place, the air thin and sharp, the sky moving faster now, scrapping and shredding clouds, scouring the stone where she stood.

ASSEMBLY REQUIRED

When I say I have her bones
I don't mean those cheekbones

Or the extended grace her ulna

Made of her leg, or the way
Her spine elongated the distance

Ribs to pelvis for a waist

Narrower than mine; rather
I mean bones being

Unlikely to shatter unless fallen on

Hard with velocity, strength
I thank her for. I could add

The bridge in our noses, a flare

And thinning, and something –
Call it wide-open

Space – behind my forehead

Where, dying, she said she will
Remain. Is that a room in my skull

With windows thrown wide, a travel

Trunk pasted with destinations,
A shame closet? Maybe

I'll never know, even when

My bones lie burned and dusted.
Still addressed to me, hers sit

Tucked under my day-bed,

My father, also boxed and sealed,
Lying beside her again.

ELEGY

From the candle
Light a candle.
Let wax fall
And burn the table.

Light the candles,
My mother said.
Scar the table,
Wish you're dead.

The dream voice said
Make memory.
My mother's dead
But speaks in me.

If art makes memory
What is this?
The poem sang me
To sleep, then vanished.

What do I call this?
Dawn won't come.
Sleep vanishes.
I wake alone.

When dawn comes
The poem still sings
Awake, alone.
If memory brings

A poem and sings her,
Let wax fall.
Memory lights me
From her candle.

3. Time and Chance

One day I woke up and knew my body

Had been colonized by bats. It had
Given itself over to an idea somehow
Involving the long haul. Not

Overnight; it came in fits

And starts then was there. You can't
Imagine how young I was, how little
I knew what I was doing, much less

My body. Decades later, my body

Hiccupped and sneezed and blew
Its pipes clean; the bats fluttered their
Own ways into the dark. It felt like that: air

Cleared like a throat, *whew*, and I could see

Land and sky meet, the vanishing
Point restoring me to myself. All that time
In between – who knows who I was,

What, if I thought, I thought I was doing.

LATE SUMMER

I hurt grass by looking, or grass
Hurts me, its pallor meaning
Tinder unless rain comes soon
Enough. Scrub oaks scale

The mountain and never get there,
Carrying torches in their hearts
To burn by. I smell dire
Tendencies, late summer laying

Its body over the foothills,
Sizzle. The sun
Sets at great length, at last
Loosing stars to fly over,

Cool-headed as always,
Blowing themselves away.

Near dawn I dreamed of Capital

-ism and woke up smelling like sugar,
Dampish, still smaller than I feel. Was I
Turning into one of those little

Old ladies we call sweet because they
Sport fanciful sneakers and hide
Stilettos in their tote bags? Mine
Sharpens up an edge fine

And whispery, a feather
You would hardly feel drawing
Your sternum open. What
You don't know don't trouble

Your head about, no worries.
Forget it's even there.

Beauty ignites,

so you wanted to
Be incandescent yourself
Or worshipping, give your
All to the flame, kindling

It with old papers then
Pages from your favorite books torn
Free – plots, poems, ideas tossed
And flown – then chair legs, the best

Table, the bed. Why not throw
Money right at it: singles, tens
Ghosting into ash. As long
As you feed it, it is too

Bright to see. Before the fire
Dies, it burns you blind.

LIFE STORIES: A Review

1 . The streaming service keeps
Popping up that movie where a young
Actor I've never heard of portrays

An icon the algorithm knows
I watch, too dead now to make movies,
Alas. The algorithm believes in my

Nostalgia, but from the preview
I know the dead actor who only ever
Played himself still does

With more life than some poor
Near look-alike kid trying to live
Up to an original.

2. This is not like
My friend grieving over the new
Sam Spade because she wanted

Clive Owen to resurrect Humphrey
Bogart. Yes, Bogart smokes
And sizzles in my head, where,

However, Hammett's words took hold
First. I say, *Give Sam a new life*
And I'll search for a role I can play

Up to, some story that comes off
Like me. When did I give up
On her? When did I settle?

When I was Joan of Arc,

Young, needing a bath, on fire. I mean
Speaking my truth to power and raising
Armies with a flick of my wrist, elect
-ricity moving my body forward. How does

Fervor appear? In error, in a flash. When
Painters wanted to paint me and poets
Sang my praises, when I imagined
Nations bent to my will or God's,

Whatever that was, when I was all my own
Sex and needed nobody else's
Touch to my illuminate my body in
-side out. Wherever did that time

Go? If I survived it. Almost in my head
I didn't consume myself with flame.

WINDOWS

In those days my head
Spoke for itself, clean
Mostly, its own entertainment

System. Behind eyes, my
Ventromedial prefrontal cortex com-

posed a self
-awareness, right out front
If it was anywhere, still there

If it is. What I did for love
I couldn't measure

Like now. A soul or something: if
I had it, the scientists didn't
Know where to look, and I

Thought nothing of it, being
Too busy looking out to care.

RETINAL EXAM

When Dr. C. shines her light
And pushes her instrument hard,

I forget myself by remembering

Newton and his crazy bodkin
Experiments and Emerson becoming

One giant eyeball for nature, *uplifted*

Into infinite space, not so
Nuts as it sounds. As usual,

Thinking helps without curing. The eye

Lit up inside looks like a ping-
pong ball, a sphere glowing red

And traced with veins popping into view

Because Dr. C. shifts them around to see
The retina clearly, which itself,

Indifferent to the same-old, catches only

Change: some bird startled up
Or lightning casting its intricate

Vanishing net across the sky. Does
My looking still the world or set it

Flying? Newton poisoned

Himself in alchemical fevers
And set his lab on fire, though story

Blames a candle and the dog

Newton named Diamond, too
Hard to melt or mint. Like the dog,

His eye came out fine, and inside

Mine everything keeps
Its slippery grip. Sometimes

Against a blank sky I make myself see

Not veins but blood cells ticker
-taping through, their pulse so regular

I count my life by them.

FROM THE OTHER SIDE

I return to a world
Burning down. How can I know,

Smoke lounging like a bad
Boyfriend all over

The furniture? For decades, I never
Considered him, but oh boy

He comes back to me now
So clearly, trailing that old

Eau de scorch. Still a noseful.
Should I search him up? No

Escape, I remember
Thinking. Never.

IF I COULD LEARN TO LOVE MY MISTAKES

Too late for that, oh well.
Meanwhile, the road to hell

Paves itself. The errors
Belong to me whatever

I may have meant back then.
Retarred again, again.

ELEGY FOR AN EX

He hated not being famous
He hated a lovely face

He never could resist
A woman smarter than he was

And would never confess
He hated hearing her voice

If he loved a little me
I loved his virility

If I can't say something nice, I say
He vanished without a trace

TEACHER, TEACHER

Even now, I catch the whiff of days
Exhausted, weather on that coast

Good, his students said,
Only after a hurricane

Or tornado. That day, he shut
His office door, lay

My poem beside his
Famous typewriter. Over forty

Years ago he reached
Both arms around me to roll

The paper in, pressed my back,
Whispered in my ear some words

Mine. Who might have sat there
Before me while he diddled

The keys, who might yet rise
And step into heavy air

Vanishing? I held myself
Perfectly still and pictured a TV

Lion lolling in his extravagant mane
While a female hauled her kill – now

I let it go. The elegy I've been
Asked for? I'll leave it

Behind too, in silence
With the poem he machined

And made his. Do I miss it?
That day, I threw it away.

Oh, to have been a girl

just
Enough older, stirring

Air and making poems
Plump with affinities, golden

And star-footed. Can I
Blame him for opening his arms

While she tripped into them? Sure,
He held her no harder than

So many in his orbit, pulling
Love as a black hole sucks

Light, cold as you
Imagine. He couldn't let go. What

Might she remember, having
Never written another poem, now

She's watched him eat others
Alive, his gravity shredding

Some to bits? See her hovering
Still on his horizon, throwing off

Hot light and pizzaz. So
Much less lucky than I was

Watching my step behind her,
She still can't escape his force.

LEVI'S ORIGINAL WAIST OVERALLS

Eighty-three years after their invention, you sat
Your ass right down on the sidewalk and left
        Days between washings, weeks, your

Defense being you didn't wear them
        Against bare parts but you did, sometimes

All of them all day, and the fabric took on your
Body's shape and motion, what might
        Rub here and touch there, swell or undo

You over decades. If, another half
        -century on, you become

        Smoother, more decorous, they do by
The same degrees and you don't notice

        Your limp coming on or side-hitch list
Or even a late straightening out, we
Can hope. Still fading, thinning, softening

        Where you work them, they fray into
Their best selves until you reach the day

        You can't live hard enough to wear them
Out, their knees and seats unspent, threads
Indigo and anything but bare.

When your fantasy unfurls

Exactly where you are
It looks like life and you
Put it on as a body can, all

Its embroideries and jewels,
Its softest flannel
Becomes you. It wears so
Well on you, you find no

Excuse to weary
And most days you don't, even
When it puts you out, grows
You old. Okay,

You tell yourself. Only
Just saying. And keep on.

SYMPTOM CHECK

Sore back. Tricky knee. Light
Flashing in the corner of my eye –
Becoming me – or a pearl
Depending, droplet

Luminating the edge
Of sight. That tooth has ached
Since I flew over the handlebars
– What, gone ten years

Now – and that itch between
My ribs I've had off-then-on
Forever, now always on. Each

Achoo and scratch-eye, a patch
Tingling my scalp. The tears,
Sure. And don't forget the rage.

FURIES

They never worked out
How to manage their hair, which

Hissed and coiled whenever
The wind blew. That was a long time

Ago, and now we've invented
Mousses, pomades – but I say buzz

-cut the vipers, no more too many
Minds of their own, each spitting

Fire and going its own way. Don't ask
Why vengeance is female; you

Should know. If only they'd had
Professional-quality clippers

And the god of the underworld
Hadn't loved them like girls

Begotten out of too much
Power and fear of the sun, "fury"

Might mean a habanero
Ice cream with bitter chocolate

And salt, delicious and too crazy
Hot to be sweet. But I doubt it.

If I had a mess of red hair,

I'd

Blaze in it, but first I'd lie
Down. If I had too many dreams
Burning me, I might die

But for what? These days I live
The edge of dream: one
Dead father and flower-lined
Path after another. Which gives

Advice, which a primrose? Whatever.
These days a man's words furl
So lightly in my ears I hardly

Need to listen. A few
Things come easy if I call.
Some won't come at all.

My head puts itself

in

The way, collides with sprung car
Trunk lids falling, cabinet
Doors I left ajar

Then forgot. I would forget it
If it weren't screwed on, the quip
Sort of goes, good thing it holds
Fast, filling my space top

-side. It trusts us
And nothing else, though a world
And its objects can pop up
Anyplace. It wants to be where

It wants. And what. There it goes
Again, I think. So it does.

VERTIGO

When my feet hold
The ground lightly I could
Fly off any second
Any handle. Not concerned

I feel the earth heft
Me over and when it lifts
Me sideways find comfort, sinews
Loosening and joints unhinging

Until my bones unstring
And dance. Once I stood
So straight the world
Took note. Infirmity came

Naturally. *Don't fall.* As you
Were, I remind myself, and am.

My dead in dreams

take it
Easy on me, dropping puns
Or tall tales or homespun
Anecdotes, offering wisdom

And directions: *Turn left*, *Don't*
Eat that, this last as usual from
My mother. One time,
I don't like telling you, she showed

Up mottled and chewed
In the wee hours–I mean visibly dis-
Composed, a state
I ignored. Why not? She kept on

Giving advice as if her condition
Was normal. By then it was.

DRAWING EXERCISE

Watch the gesture
Unbroken, sending the hand
Out, bringing it back. *Extend*

Your mind, my old teacher, now
My friend, instructs me; *let go*
The grudges you enjoy. I answer,

You should talk. You died too
Long ago. He asks, *What's left?*
A red moon smoking itself.

LINE

The ear curls and glows. One's
Freedom locks another down.
All our secrets have flown
And corners loosen their shadows.

I know how to do this alone.
So do you. We draw
Each other out. We fix
Ourselves in pen and ink.

CIRCLE

Give me one run
Around. Think

Water pebble then

Ripple as light
Emerges in time

The world keeps and lets

Us see: the now
And now until surface over

-takes us and we go.

UNDERSTANDING

Some people are more
Real than others; they
Have more ver-
isimilitude. This has been

True forever, but we didn't
Always say it. Take me
For example: you wouldn't
Tell me apart from the moon

Or that beetle on its back
Again, waving at clouds. How
Does it keep getting it
-self into that position? Why

Do I always set it
Back on its eight feet?

I returned and saw under the sun

I had no theories. No idea
What happens if time

Runs backward for no
Body I know. Heart

-break can't stop or re-
wind; the earth spins

And I dance to find
My feet. If nothing occurs

To me I sort
Exactly that, changing out

-side in. A wrinkle,
A snag, another thought

Loses itself in me, where
I may never find it.

The skull becomes literal

and boneheaded in my time,
Where else? I wake from a dream
Fleeing its shadow, beauty
I try to hold, though I see

It needs to go. All day
The *Iliad* flames a page
At a time, history flying away
Here in my head but its image

Won't burn out. Try not
Seeing it. In the afternoon ash
Falls and my mind sheds me
Like a skin it undoes

And drops, stepping out.
Okay. *Forget all that.*

NOTES

"Little Sound" owes a debt to Doug Fabrizio's *Radio West* interview with Jennifer Ackerman, September 7, 2023. The Italian "sonetto," or "little song," derives from the Latin "sonus," or "sound."

The apple flies while standing still takes its title from Anne Carson.

"Atom" was inspired in part by Jen Bervin.

Both "Photon" and "The Physicist" were inspired by Brian Greene. "Photon" is for Fred Adler.

When you invent gravity plays with Paul Virilio's famous quote, which concludes, "Every technology carries its own negativity, which is invented at the same time as technical progress."

Color has evolved more than once is for Bevil Conway, whose article on color and neurology, "Processing," gives it its first line. The painter is my friend Maureen O'Hara Ure.

"Who Sees." *Sargent and Fashion*, Tate Modern, London, 2024.

"Degas Dancers." *Les Nabis* or "The Prophets," who are thought to have ushered in early modernism, were Bonnard, Denis, Ranson, Vuillard, Roussel, Vallotton, Sérusier, Cazalis. National Gallery, London, 2023.

"Skywriting." Part 2 takes its quotes from "The Abandoned Luxury Towers That Graffiti Exposed" by Corina Knoll. *New York Times*, March 3, 2024.

"A Note on the Apparent Lowering of Moral Standards in the Lepidoptera" takes its title from that of a 1987 article on homosexual sex among butterflies by John Tennant.

I am here to stop your heart is from John Logan's film on Rothko, *Red*.

"Artichoke." Paris Botanical Garden.

"Limnology" was written at the request of textile artist Dianne Firth for her exhibition "Poetry of the Lakes." The two lakes are the Great Salt Lake in Utah (USA) and Lake George in New South Wales (AU).

"Ghost Way" was written at the request of and set (under the title "Ghost Bridge") by musician Andy Melrose for his album, *Lingerwood.*

"If My Father Dreams of Me" is for Jamie Smith, who asked me if the dead think of us.

"Three Dreams." For Mark Strand, Larry Levis, and William Coles.

The day eighty. After "Wallace Stevens Comes Back to Read His Poems at the 92nd Street Y," by Mark Strand.

"Family Snaps" is for my brothers.

"Comedy." Dante, *The Divine Comedy.*

"Elegy." "Art is memory made public." David Mitchell

"Retinal Exam." "There I feel that nothing can befall me in life—no disgrace, no calamity, (leaving me my eyes,) which nature cannot repair." Emerson

"Teacher, Teacher." The discarded poem was "The Seismologist's Daughter."

"Levi's Original Waist Overalls." Shrink-to-Fit 501s: 1890, 1973, 2023.

"Circle." Picasso said, "Style is the difference between a circle and the way you draw it."

I returned and saw under the sun. From *Ecclesiastes.*

ACKNOWLEDGMENTS

Journals:

DIAGRAM: "Levi's Original Waist Overalls," "Symptom Check." *Gargoyle*: "Not One Thing," "Degas Dancers," "Artichokes." *Image*: "Advent." *Sugarhouse Review*: "Family Snaps," "Beauty," "If My Father Dreams of Me." upstreet: *One day I woke up and knew my body, The apple flies while standing still. Western Humanities Review*: "Little Sound," "Elegy," "Sestina in Prose" (as part of the lyric essay on poetics, "Resurrection Dreaming").

Invited/commissioned poems:

When I was Joan of Arc and "Still Living in My Head." *Creative Writing Responses to Images of the Living Brain*. Ed. Julia Prendergast, Jen Webb, Eileen Herbert-Goodall.

If past becomes future. The Gift of Animals: Poems of Love, Loss, & Connection. Ed. Alison Hawthorne Deming.

"Limnology." *Poetry and the Lakes*," Dianne Firth (textile artist). Exhibition October 2024, Canberra AU.

"Comedy." For *Divining Dante*. Ed. Paul Munden and Nessa O'Mahoney.

"Ghost Way" (as "Ghost Bridge"). *Lingerwood* (album). Music by Andrew Melrose.

"Relic." For *Remnant*. Ed. Cassandra Atherton.

ABOUT THE AUTHOR

Katharine Coles is a Distinguished Professor at the University of Utah, where she teaches courses in creative writing, poetry, and poetics. She has received grants and awards from The Guggenheim Foundation, the US National Science Foundation's Antarctic Artists and Writer Program, the National Endowment for the Arts, and the National Endowment for the Humanities. *Time and Chance* is her tenth collection of poems.